LeMoyne Stars Made Easy

by Sharyn Squier Craig

CHITRA PUBLICATIONS

Your Best Value in Quilting!

All Rights Reserved. Published in United States of America
Printed in China

Chitra Publications
2 Public Avenue
Montrose, Pennsylvania 18801

Fourth printing: 2003
Library of Congress Cataloging-in-Publication Data

Craig, Sharyn Squier, 1947-
    LeMoyne stars made easy / by Sharyn Squier Craig.
       p. cm.
    ISBN 1-885588-19-4
    1. Patchwork. 2. Patchwork--Patterns. 3. Quilting. 4. Quilting-
-Patterns.   5. Star quilts.   6. Stars in art.   I. Title.
TT835.C7332 1998
746.46'041--dc21   97-48541
                                   CIP

Editors: Nancy Roberts and Joyce Libal
Design and Illustrations: Kimberly L. Grace
Cover Photography: Guy Cali Associates, Inc., Clarks Summit, PA
Inside Photography: Ken Jacques Photography, San Diego, CA
Craige's Studio, Montrose, PA
Guy Cali Associates Inc., Clarks Summit

Our Mission Statement

We publish quality quilting magazines and books that recognize, promote and inspire self-expression. We are dedicated to serving our customers with respect, kindness and efficiency.

Table of Contents

Acknowledgements:

A book like this one, which features lots of quilts, is only possible with help from my friends and students. Throughout my 19-year quiltmaking and teaching career, I've been fortunate to be able to "fine tune" my ideas, class hand-outs and methods by using them with students. My heartfelt thanks to the following quiltmakers who put their current projects aside in order to piece many of the quilts you see in this book:

Sandy Andersen	*Barbara Hutchins*	*Nancy Nichols*
Ruth Gordy	*Lynn Johnson*	*Linda Packer*
Stevii Graves	*Laurine Leeke*	*Margret Reap*
Linda Hamby	*Harriet Love*	*Carol Shumaik*
Diane Harrington	*Mary Jo Manzuk*	*Carolyn Smith*
Marilyn Henderson	*Pat Marean*	*Regina Spurgeon*
Louise Hixon	*Kathy Nelson*	*Arlene Stamper*

Special thanks to Joanie Keith who enhances so many of my quilts with her special machine quilting.

"Even you are going to have to hand piece this block!"

I'll never forget when my adult education instructor spoke those words back in 1978. She was talking about a LeMoyne Star block with set-in pieces. At that time most piecing was done by hand, but I learned early on how to use my sewing machine to save time and sew accurate blocks. So, my teacher's words provided just the challenge I needed!

The block is made up of diamonds, triangles and squares. Because of the angles, some of the pieces need to be set-in, a quiltmaking technique of joining pieces where three seams come together. This task requires some skill in order to make the block lie flat. So when my teacher implied that machine piecing the LeMoyne Star was not possible, I set out to find a way to do it.

It took many attempts before I finally succeeded in sewing an acceptable Star block that laid flat and had all eight diamonds meeting precisely in the center. I call my method of construction Y-seaming and it's somewhat different from the usual setting-in techniques that require difficult fabric manipulation and pivoting. In fact, you'll find Y-seaming is an easy alternative to most setting-in methods.

I suggest that you begin with a simple 6" LeMoyne Star. You'll find both directions for cutting with templates and rotary cutting dimensions for it in the first chapter. Using templates with your rotary cutter is covered there, too. If you have never tried this before, I think you'll be pleasantly surprised at the results. Make one block to be sure pieces are cut accurately and sewn with an exact 1/4" seam allowance before cutting out pieces for an entire quilt.

When you are comfortable that your Star block "works," cut pieces for lots of 6" LeMoyne Stars. Once they are cut out, you're more likely to sew them together whenever you have small amounts of time. It won't be long before you have enough for a quilt. It takes me about 15 minutes to sew one block. That means I can have a block sewn in the time it takes to boil spaghetti! Being organized helps. I keep cut pieces in a sturdy, labeled shirt box so I can find them quickly when I have a few minutes to sew.

I'll walk you through using Y-seaming in a 6" LeMoyne Star in Chapter 2. You'll find the simple diagrams and step-by-step photos highlight the important points from cutting to construction.

Once you master Y-seaming, look over the other blocks in Chapter 3 for which you can use this technique. "LeMoyne Star and Friends" (page 10) is a great way to try out all of the different blocks, and end up with a sampler quilt when you're through.

Then get starry-eyed over the quilts in the gallery on page 16. They'll give you lots of ideas for setting the blocks together. Explore the idea of substitution. For example, replace North Star blocks with Carpenter's Wheel blocks if they are your favorites. If piecing one of the more complex blocks is enough, frame it in a medallion set. You'll see these ideas and more in Chapter 4. Do you want to make Star blocks in other sizes? The drafting information in Chapter 5 can help.

I hope you like the easy set-up of this book. It's meant to provide maximum information in the most useful way. Begin to use it now and you'll soon be on your way to the stars!

Sharyn

CHAPTER 1

Quick-Cutting Block Pieces from Strips

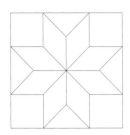

We'll start with a 6" LeMoyne Star. It has three pattern pieces—a 1 3/4" square, a 1 3/4" right triangle and a 1 3/4" diamond. Use pattern pieces 1A (page 26), 2A and 3A (page 28). I prefer cutting pieces using templates and a rotary cutter. Does this surprise you? Many quilters think that you must cut with scissors when you use templates. This is not true. The following instructions will show you how easy it is to cut accurate pieces using both. If you prefer no-template cutting, you'll find the dimensions you need and cutting instructions for this method as well.

PREPARING THE TEMPLATES

You can make sturdy templates for use with a rotary cutter. You'll need paper, translucent heavyweight template plastic, a glue stick and heavyweight sandpaper. You'll also need scissors for cutting plastic and sandpaper.
•   Trace or draw the pattern pieces on unlined paper. Or, you may prefer to have them photocopied at 100%.
•   Glue the template plastic to the right side of the pattern pieces.
•   Turn the pattern pieces over and glue the sandpaper to the back, rough side out.
•   Let the three layers dry for at least 10 minutes to prevent them from shifting when you cut the pieces out.
•   Cut each piece out on the cutting line.
    Or, you may wish to purchase the John Flynn Cut-Your-Own-Template Kit and simply cut pattern pieces using its instructions. (See ordering information on page 6.)

Cutting Without Templates
These directions take proper grainline into account.

Pattern Piece (& how many to cut)	Finished Size	Cutting Size	Cutting Diagram
Square (4)	1 3/4"	2 1/4"	
Right triangle (4)	1 3/4" sides	3 3/4" square;	then cut it in quarters diagonally
45° Diamond (8)	1 3/4"	1 3/4"	

CUTTING FABRIC STRIPS

Each LeMoyne Star block requires four squares cut from background fabric, four right triangles cut from background fabric and eight diamonds cut from one or more fabrics. Begin by cutting selvage-to-selvage fabric strips whether you plan to cut with or without templates. Just follow these instructions to cut fabric strips in the following widths.

Strip sizes:
•   For the squares, cut 2 1/4"-wide strips of background fabric.
•   For the triangles, cut 1 7/8"-wide strips of background fabric if you will be using templates.
NOTE: *If you are cutting without templates, cut these strips 3 3/4"-wide.*
•   For the diamonds, cut 1 3/4"-wide strips from star fabrics.

Cutting fabric strips:
•   Fold the fabric selvage to selvage and smooth it. Then fold it to the selvages again. The fabric is now in four layers.

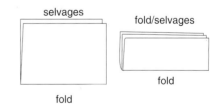

•   Place the fabric on the cutting mat, as shown for right- or left-handed cutting.

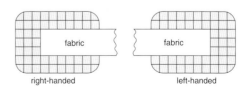

•   Place the folded edge of the fabric on a horizontal line of the mat. Position the ruler on a vertical line of the mat, above the uneven edges of the fabric so that a small amount of fabric extends beyond the cutting edge of the ruler. Careful positioning of the fabric and ruler with the lines of the mat will ensure cutting straight strips. Even the fabric by cutting along the edge of the ruler.

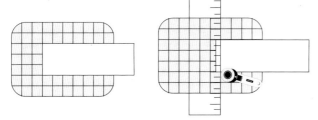

• Measuring from the trimmed edge, move the ruler over and cut strips the required width through all four layers of fabric. You'll find this is an efficient way to cut pieces for the block because there are four layers of fabric and you need pieces in multiples of four.

Cutting Squares:

• Trim the end of a 2 1/4"-wide folded strip, removing the selvages and the fold.
• Position the square template on the strips and cut along the edge. There's no need to measure or remember numbers. Simply position the template and cut.

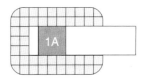

• To cut squares without templates, place the ruler on the strip, measure 2 1/4" from the trimmed edge and cut.

Cutting Triangles:

• Place a 1 7/8"-wide folded strip on the cutting mat. Working from the open end, position the triangle template on the strip so that the long edge is closest to you. Cut carefully around the template.

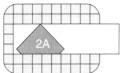

• Flip the template over, placing it on the strip next to the cut-out area, and cut four more triangles. Continue in this manner until you have cut as many triangles from the strip as possible, or until you have as many as you need. Remember, each block requires four triangles and you are cutting them in sets of four. If you are making one block, this means you need to cut only once to make enough triangles.
• To cut without templates, trim the end of a folded 3 3/4"-wide strip, removing the selvages and fold. Measure 3 3/4" from the trimmed edge and cut.
• Cut the squares in quarters diagonally. Be careful when making the second cut because the triangles tend to shift. This will provide 16 triangles—enough for four blocks.

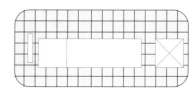

Cutting Diamonds:

• Place a 1 3/4"-wide folded strip on the cutting mat. Beginning at the open end, position the diamond template on the strip and cut along the two sides. This makes four diamonds. That's enough for one block if you are using two different fabrics. Either cut 4 more diamonds from a second fabric, or cut again from this strip if you want all 8 diamonds to match.

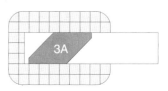

• To cut without templates, place a 1 3/4"-wide folded strip on the cutting mat. Position your ruler on the strip so that the 45° angle is aligned with the long edge of the strip. Cut along the edge of the ruler, creating an angled edge on the strip.

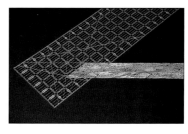

• Measure 1 3/4" from the angled edge and cut. Cut again if using 8 diamonds from one fabric, or cut 4 diamonds from a second fabric.

NOTE: Because cutting accurately is so important, I recommend cutting the diamonds without templates for experienced quilters only. Often construction problems can be traced to inaccurate cutting, but you shouldn't have that problem if you use templates.

CHAPTER 2

Welcome to Y-Seaming!

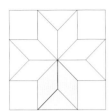

Now you have the pieces for one or more 6" LeMoyne Star blocks. So let's piece them using Y-seaming! Why not sew the block by following the step-by-step photos right at your sewing machine? Set up your machine with cotton thread, a size 12/80 needle (a medium size for regular sewing) and an open-toed or straight stitch foot so you can see your sewing better. Sewing an accurate 1/4" seam is important. If you don't have a special 1/4"-foot on your machine, see "Guaranteed Stitching Accuracy" for some tips.

It helps to think of the block as being made up of sub-units. This is true of the LeMoyne Star and all of the blocks in Chapter 3. Begin sewing the smallest sub-units first.

Guaranteed Stitching Accuracy

Here's an easy way to make sure you sew precise 1/4" seams.

• Place a small strip-cutting ruler under the presser foot of your sewing machine.
• Slowly turn the hand wheel until the needle comes down exactly on the line that is 1/4" from the edge of the ruler.
• Lower the presser foot to secure the ruler.
• Place a barrier guide on the throat plate at the right, along the ruler's edge. I use small strips cut from Dr. Scholls® Foot and Shoe Padding, an adhesive material available in drugstores. Or you could adhere masking tape to the throat plate as a guide. The raw edges of the fabric pieces should just touch the barrier guide as you feed them through the machine.

Here's another option. Do you have a quilting bar guide attachment for your sewing machine? If so, just attach it according to manufacturer's directions. Secure the ruler under the presser foot as described before. Then position the bar guide so it is aligned with the edge of the ruler. Remove the ruler and the bar will be the guide.

SEWING THE BLOCK
• Lay out the pieces for the first sub-unit near your sewing machine, as shown. Stack the matching pieces for the remaining three sub-units on top of the first.

• Keeping the triangle on top, sew from edge to edge, toward the blunted point of the triangle. (*Note:* If you cut without templates, the triangles will not be bunted.) Do not clip the threads or remove the pieces from the machine yet.
• Repeat with the remaining three triangles and diamonds, chain sewing them.

• Pick up one triangle and place it on top of the diamond at the left, right sides together and two edges aligned.

• Clip the units apart and finger press each seam allowance toward the diamond by running your thumbnail along the ridge of the seam allowance. Stack pieced units in the same position they were in before sewing.

TIP!

Remember, the first seam of a Y-seam is always sewn from edge to edge.

- Working with the pieces for one sub-unit, place the remaining diamond right sides together with the triangle in the pieced unit, matching edges as before.

- Turn the pieces over so that the triangle is on top and you can see the previous seamline. Sew from the blunted point of the triangle to the seamline and stop. Lock the stitches by sewing in place or backstitching two or three stitches.
- Repeat with remaining units, finger pressing seam allowances toward diamonds.

- Place the diamonds of one sub-unit right sides together, pulling the triangle down and out of the way.

- To complete the sub-unit and the first Y-seam, sew the diamonds together from the outer point to the seamline and lock the stitches as before. (*Note:* You may prefer to sew this seam from the seamline to the blunted point of the triangle. Try both ways and see which one works best for you. Your decision may be based on visibility and the type of presser foot you are using.)

- Repeat to complete four sub-units. Finger press the seam allowances toward the diamond added last (at the right in the sub-unit). The arrows in the photo show the directions seam allowances should lie in the sub-unit.

- Stack the sub-units with the triangle closest to you. Stack the squares at the right, four layers deep.

- Take one square and place it on top of a sub-unit, right sides together and corners aligned. Keeping the square on top, sew from edge to edge. Leave pieces in the machine and do not clip threads yet.
- Repeat with the remaining squares and sub-units, chain sewing them.

- Clip the units apart and finger press the seam allowances toward the squares.
- Place these units next to each other in two piles of two units each, as shown.

- Place the unit at the upper right on top of the unit below it, right sides together and corners aligned. Turn the units over so that the square is on top. Sew from the outer edge toward the seamline, joining the units. Stop sewing at the seamline and lock the stitches.
- Repeat with the remaining two units. Finger press the seam allowances toward the squares.

- Position the diamonds in one pair of these joined units right sides together, matching corners and aligning seam allowances. This should be easy because seams will butt together naturally from finger pressing. Fold the square down, out of the way.

- Sew the diamonds together from seamline to seamline to complete a half-star section, locking stitches at both ends of the seam. Repeat with the remaining joined unit.

- Turn the half-star sections right side up and finger press the seam allowances toward the diamonds at the right.

- To join the half-star sections, place the square of one unit on the diamond adjacent to it in the other unit, right sides together. Keeping the square on top, stitch from the edge to the seamline. Stop and lock the stitches.
- Repeat to stitch the remaining square to the adjacent diamond.
- You are ready to complete the final seam at the center of the block. Place the half-star sections right sides together, carefully matching the mid-points of the star. Adjust the diamonds as necessary to make sure the seam allowances match. The finger pressing you did earlier will help here because the seam allowances alternate directions, allowing you to butt the seams neatly together.
- Set your machine for a longer, basting stitch. Sew about six stitches through the center. Remove the block from the machine and check for alignment.

- When you are satisfied that the seams match and the points are sharp, shorten the stitch length. Sew the block center from seamline to seamline, locking stitches at both ends of the seam.

- Fan the seam allowances at the center by working them with your fingers so that all seam allowances lie in the same direction (clockwise around the center point), making the block lie perfectly flat. Press the block with a hot iron.

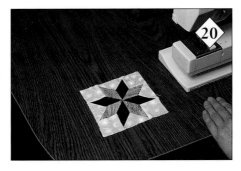

Congratulations! Your first block made with Y-seaming is finished.

Now cut and piece a second, a third and a fourth block. Not only are they fun to make, the practice will also help you become completely comfortable with the Y-seaming method. Here's the bonus—as you practice, you'll create a collection of these 6" LeMoyne Star blocks. I've found they come in handy so often when I'm designing and assembling quilts. I've used them as spacer blocks, cornerstones in sashing and in borders. I've even used them alone in quilts! You'll see them in several quilts in the gallery that begins on page 16.

CHAPTER 3

Starring the Star Blocks

▼ *This beautiful **"LeMoyne Star and Friends"** sampler (72" square) showcases all 12 blocks that you can make with the Y-seaming instructions and patterns in this book! Can you find* 16 of the 6" LeMoyne Star blocks like those you learned to piece in Chapter 2? A dozen are used in the setting and four are joined to make a 12" block. I told you they were versatile!

Row 1, from left: **Festival Star, Star of the Magi**

Row 2, from left: **Rolling Star, Morning Star, Virginia Star**

Row 3, from left: **Carpenter's Wheel, LeMoyne Star** (four 6" blocks)

Row 4, from left: **Flying Swallows, North Star, Striped Star**

Row 5, from left: **Snow Crystal, Blazing Star**

Guy Cali Associattes Inc.

General Directions:

Here are a dozen beautiful Star blocks, each given in two sizes. Except for the small LeMoyne Star which you pieced in the previous chapter, each block is given in both 10 1/4" and 12" finished block sizes. Although the two sizes of the LeMoyne Star block are smaller than the others (5 1/8" and 6" finished), I've kept the scale similar so you can use all of these Star blocks together. I suggest sewing four of the smaller blocks together to make one 10 1/4" or 12" block as I did in "LeMoyne Star and Friends." Festival Star is also given in a bonus 11" size because the 6" LeMoyne Star block fits perfectly in the center of it. You may wish to use a 6" block you already pieced and simply sew the remaining pieces to it to turn it into a Festival Star.

The pattern pieces for all of the blocks begin on page 26. Templates are marked with both letters and numbers. Templates marked "A" are for 6" LeMoyne Star blocks and other Star blocks measuring 12". "B" templates are for 5 1/8" LeMoyne Star blocks and other Star blocks measuring 10 1/4". The two "C" templates are the bonus ones for the 11" Festival Star. Numbers correspond to shapes used in the blocks. Where it's important to know, arrows on block diagrams will indicate straight of grain. When possible, rotary cutting dimensions are also listed with each block in case you prefer to cut some shapes this way.

As with the LeMoyne Star, identify the sub-units to determine piecing order. The Striped Star, Morning Star, Virginia Star and North Star are easy—simply piece the diamonds and then sew the block just like you sewed the LeMoyne Star. For Blazing Star, piece the diamonds, corner squares and triangles and then assemble the block as for the LeMoyne Star. You'll use Y-seams to piece the diamonds in Flying Swallows and then complete the block as before. The remaining five blocks are more complex and have several sub-units within the design. However, none require more than five pattern pieces. Sub-unit diagrams will guide you when piecing them.

TIP! *To determine how wide to cut fabric strips for cutting pattern pieces, make the template and then measure it. Measure a triangle from its base to the top. You may be surprised to find that the strip width for cutting diamonds will often measure the same as their finished dimensions.*

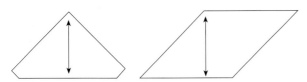

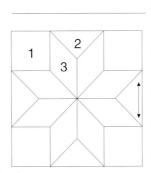

LeMoyne Star

Use Pattern Pieces 1, 2 and 3

Or use these dimensions that include seam allowances to cut some pieces in these block sizes:

	Square #1	Triangle #2	Diamond #3
6"	2 1/4"	Cut a 3 3/4" square in quarters diagonally	1 3/4"
5 1/8"	2"	Use template	Use template

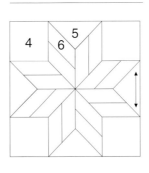

Striped Star

Use Pattern Pieces 4, 5 and 6

Or use these dimensions that include seam allowances to cut some pieces in these block sizes:

	Square #4	Triangle #5
12"	4"	Cut a 6 1/4" square in quarters diagonally
10 1/4"	3 1/2"	Cut a 5 1/2" square in quarters diagonally

TIP! *To save time, sew two fabric strips together. Then use diamond pattern piece #10 to cut diamonds from the pieced strips.*

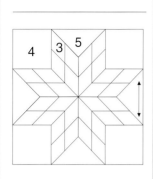
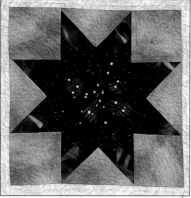

Morning Star

Use Pattern Pieces 3, 4 and 5

Or use these dimensions that include seam allowances to cut some pieces in these block sizes:

	Diamond #3	Square #4	Triangle #5
12"	1 3/4"	4"	Cut a 6 1/4" square in quarters diagonally
10 1/4"	Use template	3 1/2"	Cut a 5 1/2" square in quarters diagonally

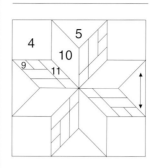

North Star

Use Pattern Pieces 4, 5, 9, 10 and 11

Or use these dimensions that include seam allowances to cut some pieces in these block sizes:

	Square #4	Triangle #5	Diamond #10
12"	4"	Cut a 6 1/4" square in quarters diagonally	3"
10 1/4"	3 1/2"	Cut a 5 1/2" square in quarters diagonally	Use template

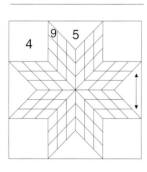

Virginia Star

Use Pattern Pieces 4, 5 and 9

Or use these dimensions that include seam allowances to cut some pieces in these block sizes:

	Square #4	Triangle #5	Diamond #9
12"	4"	Cut a 6 1/4" square in quarters diagonally	Use template
10 1/4"	3 1/2"	Cut a 5 1/2" square in quarters diagonally	Use template

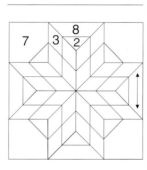

Blazing Star

Use Pattern Pieces 2, 3, 7, and 8

Or use these dimensions that include seam allowances to cut some pieces in these block sizes:

	Triangle #2	Diamond #3
12"	2 5/8" square cut in half diagonally	1 3/4"
10 1/4"	2 3/8" square cut in half diagonally	Use template

TIP!

This Virginia Star block is related to the Lone Star. You can easily adapt your favorite Lone Star strip-piecing technique to it. Once you piece a Virginia Star, you can use the same methods to make a Lone Star quilt in any size you wish, with any number of small diamonds!

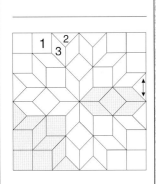

Carpenter's Wheel

Piecing Guidelines

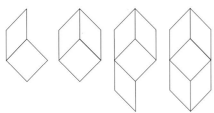

Center Unit-Make 4

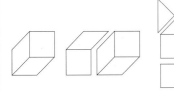
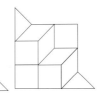

Corner Unit-Make 4

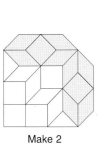

Make 2

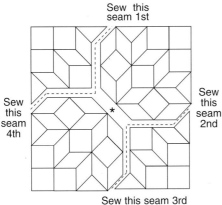

Sew this seam 1st

Sew this seam 4th

Sew this seam 2nd

Sew this seam 3rd

* Close up this seam last

Use Pattern Pieces 1, 2 and 3
Or use these dimensions that include seam allowances to cut some pieces in these block sizes:

	Square #1	Triangle #2	Diamond #3
12"	2 1/4"	Cut a 3 3/4" square in quarters diagonally	1 3/4"
10 1/4"	2"	Use template	Use template

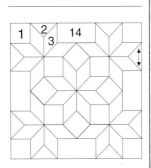

Snow Crystal

Piecing Guidelines

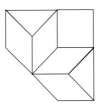

Corner Unit-
Make 4

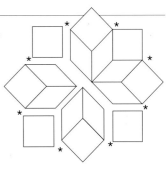

Center Unit-Make 1
* Stop sewing 1/4" from the raw edges of each seam where two squares join. This will make it easier to sew the diamonds.

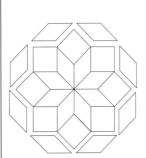

It may help to sew with the diamonds on top for more control.

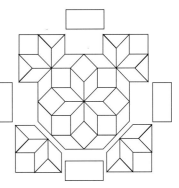

Sew the long sides of the rectangles, seamline to seamline. Close up the short seams of each rectangle.

Use Pattern Pieces 1, 2, 3 and 14
Or use these dimensions that include seam allowances to cut some pieces in these block sizes:

	Square #1	Triangle #2	Diamond #3
12"	2 1/4"	Cut a 3 3/4" square in quarters diagonally	1 3/4"
10 1/4"	2"	Use template	Use template

	Rectangle #14
12"	2 1/4" x 4"
10 1/4"	2" x 3 1/2"

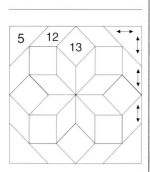

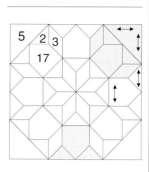

Rolling Star
Piecing Guidelines

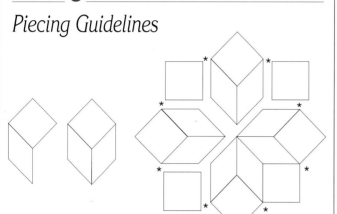

* Stop sewing 1/4" from the raw edges of each seam where two squares join. This will make it easier to sew the diamonds.

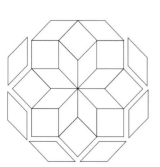

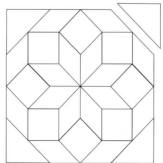

Use Pattern Pieces 5, 12 and 13
Or use these dimensions that include seam allowances to cut some pieces in these block sizes:

	Triangle #5	Diamond #12	Square #13
12"	Cut a 4 3/8" square in half diagonally	2 1/4"	3"
10 1/4"	Cut a 3 7/8" square in half diagonally	2"	2 5/8"

Star of the Magi
Piecing Guidelines

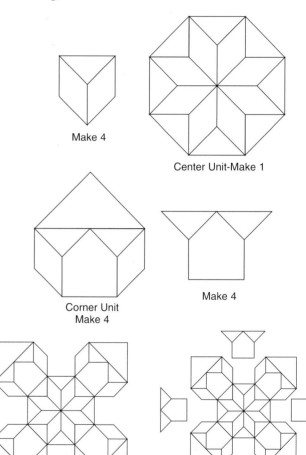

Make 4

Center Unit-Make 1

Corner Unit
Make 4

Make 4

Use Pattern Pieces 2, 3, 5, and 17
Or use these dimensions that include seam allowances to cut some pieces in these block sizes:

	Small Triangle #2	Diamond #3	Large Triangle #5
12"	2 5/8" square cut in half diagonally	1 3/4"	Cut a 4 3/8" square in half diagonally
10 1/4"	2 3/8" square cut in half diagonally	Use template	Cut a 3 7/8" square in half diagonally

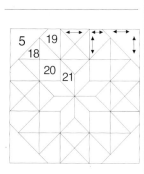

Festival Star

Piecing Guidelines

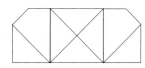

Make 4   Make 2

Make 2

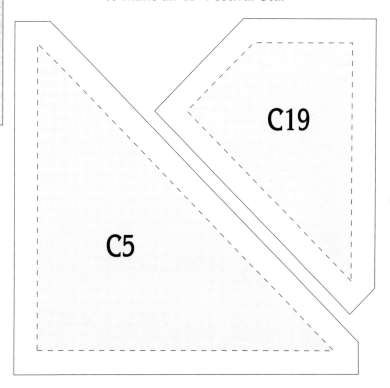

C5

C19

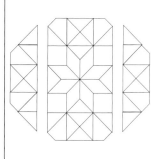

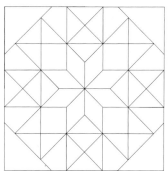

Use Pattern Pieces 5, 18, 19, 20 and 21

Or use these dimensions that include seam allowances to cut some pieces in these block sizes:

	Triangle #5
12"	cut a 4 3/8" square in half diagonally
10 1/4"	cut a 3 7/8" square in half diagonally

BONUS BLOCK! 11" Festival Star

Use Pattern Pieces A1, A2, A3, C5 and C19

Or use these dimensions that include seam allowances to cut some pieces in these block sizes:

Large Triangle	Small Triangle	Square	Diamond
Cut a 4 1/8" square in half diagonally	Cut a 3 1/4" square in quarters diagonally	2 1/4"	1 3/4"

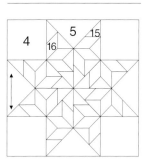

Flying Swallows

Use Pattern Pieces 4, 5, 15 and 16

Or use these dimensions that include seam allowances to cut some pieces in these block sizes:

	Square #4	Large Triangle #5	Small Triangle #15
12"	4"	Cut a 6 1/4" square in quarters diagonally	Use template
10 1/4"	3 1/2"	Cut a 5 1/2" square in quarters diagonally	Cut a 3" square in quarters diagonally

◄ *When the friendship blocks for my* **"North Star"** *quilt (66" square) were not all the same size, I framed them with light strips and added accent triangles in the corners.*

►*Pat Marean used blocks from the same exchange in her* **"Luminous North Star"** *(54" x 66"). She set them on point and pieced the setting triangles to add further design interest.*

▶ *Blocks are set on point with triple-lattice sashing in my* **"Plaid Stars, Rolling Stars"** *(79" x 103"). Smaller LeMoyne Star blocks are the cornerstones in the sashing.*

◀ *I combined 5 1/8" LeMoyne Star blocks with 10 1/4" Morning Star blocks in this Morning Star quilt (52" square). Lots of my quilting friends helped meet a deadline by piecing the blocks for this project.*

▲ ▼ *Linda Packer used the same setting and similar colors in her North Star and Virginia Star quilts (both 40" square) just to see how using different blocks impacts the design.*

◀ *Why not use four Star blocks in a wallhanging like Carolyn Smith did in her Blazing Star quilt (33" square)?*

▶ *Arlene Stamper enlarged a Carpenter's Wheel block and faceted the large diamonds into smaller ones. The result is this Broken Star quilt (115" square). Try the same thing with other blocks found in Chapter 3.*

◀ *"Snow Crystal Express" (72" square) is composed of 12" blocks set with triple-lattice sashing. I used 6" LeMoyne Star blocks as cornerstones.*

◄ In "Jewel of LeMoyne" (48" square) I set Sandy Andersen's blocks together using sashing cut from the same fabrics as the background in the blocks. It makes the blocks appear to "float." They are grounded by the jewel-tone cornerstones.

◄ ▲ Medallion settings work beautifully for a single Star block. I designed the medallion corners and pieced the center blocks. Then Margret Reap took it from there to experiment with color and complete these quilts which have the same set. "Star of the Magi" and "Carpenter's Wheel Medallion" (30" square).

▶The 6"-wide sashing in my **"Festival Star"** (72" square) is composed of a narrow dark center stip and wider light strips. I used a variety of fabrics in the sashing and the borders.

▲ Inspired by an antique quilt, I set the LeMoyne Star blocks in a Double Irish Chain in **"LeMoyne Star on the Double"** (40"square).

▼ I broke large diamonds into small ones in this Snow Crystal quilt I call **"Crystalization"** (31" square).

CHAPTER 4

Setting Solutions

You've mastered Y-seaming and stitched an assortment of beautiful Star blocks. Now have some design fun by setting them together into a quilt top. Let's explore some options!

Examples of standard settings are described and illustrated here. Part of this chapter is devoted to coloration. Color choices *can make such surprising differences in a finished quilt. If you feel hesitant about set and color decisions, here's my secret—turn the challenge into fun! That way you can relax and enjoy the designing process.*

STANDARD SETTING OPTIONS

1) The tangent set, also known as the side-by-side set, is perhaps the most familiar way to set blocks together. They can be joined in a straight set or a diagonal one. The tangent set is often used for repetitive block designs where the same block is used throughout the quilt. It is less frequently used in samplers. It can be one of the easiest ways to set blocks together if the blocks are all the same size.

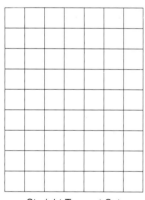
Straight Tangent Set

Diagonal Tangent Set

Diagonal sets require side and corner setting triangles. It's important to cut these triangles so that straight grain is on the outside edges of the quilt to avoid stretching or distortion. Use the handy chart on this page to rotary cut setting triangles for 16 different block sizes, from mini to medallion-size.

If you are working with block sizes other than those listed, here's how to determine the size to cut each type of setting triangle:
• For side setting triangles, the straight grain needs to be on the long side of each triangle. It's best to cut a square, then cut it in quarters diagonally to keep the grain in the correct place. Each square will yield four side setting triangles. To determine the size square to cut, multiply the finished size of the block times 1.414. Add 1 1/4" (1.25) to the result, round it up to the nearest 1/8" if necessary to make a number that is easy to work with and cut a square this size. Then slice the square from corner to corner in both directions.
• For corner setting triangles, the straight grain needs to be along the two short sides of each. Cut a square, then cut it in half diagonally to yield two corner setting triangles. To deter-

mine the size square to cut, divide the finished size of the block by 1.414 and add 7/8" (0.875). Round up to the nearest 1/8" and cut a square this size. Then slice it from corner to corner.

Dimensions for Cutting Setting Triangles

Finished Block Size	Cut Square Size for Corner Triangles	Cut Square Size for Side Triangles
2"	2 3/8"	4 1/8"
3"	3"	5 1/2"
4"	3 3/4"	7"
5"	4 1/2"	8 3/8"
6"	5 1/8"	9 3/4"
7"	5 7/8"	11 1/4"
8"	6 5/8"	12 5/8"
9"	7 1/4"	14"
10"	8"	15 1/2"
10 1/4"	8 1/8"	15 3/4"
12"	9 3/8"	18 1/4"
14"	10 7/8"	21 1/8"
16"	12 1/4"	23 7/8"
18"	13 5/8"	26 3/4"
20"	15 1/8"	29 5/8"
24"	17 7/8"	35 1/4"

2) An alternating set with plain squares, set straight or diagonally, works well when you want a larger quilt without having to piece a lot more blocks. To keep the overall design balanced in a straight set, an uneven number of rows works best.

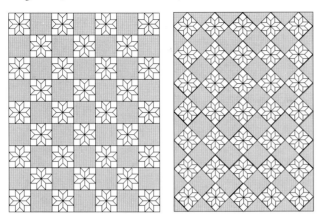

3) An alternating set with a connector block is similar to the previous set, except that the alternating square is a pieced block rather than a plain square of fabric. The connector block is often a simple pattern as seen in these blocks:

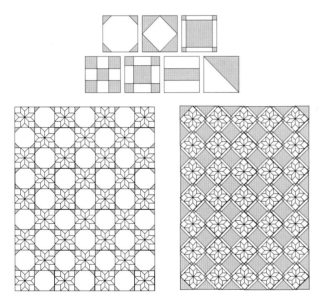

4) Sashed sets have fabric strips stitched between the blocks. Sashing increases the size of the quilt and can provide visual relief (a resting place for the eyes) in the overall design. Many blocks look better when separated by sashing rather than set tangent. You can add color and interest by using cornerstones (small squares), cut from a different fabric than the sashing, at the intersections between blocks.

As a guide, single strips of sashing generally measure 1/4 of the finished block size. This means that sashing for 12" finished blocks would be 3" wide (cut size 3 1/2").

Consider pieced sashing, too. It can be simple or elaborate, depending on the blocks. When you piece the sashing, the pieced strip can be wider than 1/4 of the finished block. For example, "Snow Crystal Express" (page 19) and "Plaid Stars,

Rolling Stars" (page 17) both use 6"-wide sashing successfully. If the strips weren't pieced, the 6" width could have overpowered the blocks.

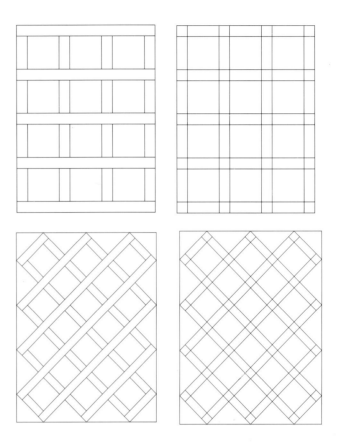

TIP!

To determine the size of side- and corner-setting triangles for a diagonally set sashed quilt, you'll need to consider the

Corner triangle= Block size plus the width of two sashing strips

Side triangle= Block size plus the width of one sashing strip

width of the sashing. Side triangles increase in size by the width of one sashing strip. For them, add the finished width of the sashing to the finished block size. Multiply this number by 1.414 and add 1 1/4" to the result. Round the number up to the nearest 1/8" and cut a square this size. Corner triangles increase in size by the width of two sashing strips. For them, multiply the finished width of the sashing by two and add it to the finished block size. Divide this number by 1.414, add 7/8" and round up as before.

5) Framed blocks have a border around them, just as a painting does. It can be simple, complex, narrow or wide. You can use a frame to create an on-point look, as in a square-in-a-square. You can frame blocks on just two sides, as in an Attic Window. You can even use framing strips to set odd-size blocks together successfully, as described in my book *Twist 'n Turn* (Chitra Publications, 1996).

When working with odd-size blocks, consider sewing on framing strips cut wide enough to make the block a size that's easy to work with.

6. In a medallion set, a single block or pieced design is placed at the center of the quilt top, then framed with triangles and one or more borders. The framing pieces may be pieced or cut from a single fabric. Medallion sets are particularly appealing for these Star blocks, because each one can be so striking and dramatic when used alone in a quilt. A medallion set is a perfect way to use such one-of-a-kind blocks in a quilt. Try this set, framing the Star block with pieced triangles such as those shown in the examples.

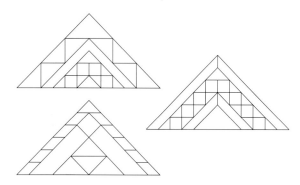

It's easy to design your own pieced triangles for a medallion set. You'll need graph paper, a pencil and a ruler. I prefer using tablets of 17" x 22" four-squares-to-the-inch graph paper. It's helpful if the paper has darkened lines at one-inch intervals. Art supply stores are a good source for this type of graph paper. Then just follow these steps:
• Draw a line on the graph paper equal to the finished size of the block you are framing, for example 12". This is the base of the triangle.

• Find the mid-point of the line and place a dot there. In this case, place a dot on the line at 6".

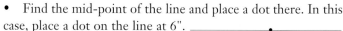

• Measure up from the midpoint and mark a dot on the paper at a point equal to the midpoint measurement. In this case, 6".

• Connect this dot to each end of the base. This is the finished size of the triangle you need to frame the block.

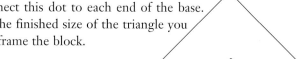

• Now draw lines to divide the triangle into squares, rectangles and triangles. Try several different ways to divide the triangle until you find the one that works best with your quilt block.

Think about color!
Most of the setting options allow you to be creative in choosing colors to emphasize or soften the impact of your quilt blocks. Often, when I finish blocks and look at them together, I feel as if something is missing from the quilt. This can happen even when I've made them with a particular color scheme in mind. Introducing one or more new colors in the borders, sashing, connector blocks or framing pieces can make a big difference. Here are some tips that will help you as you work with settings:
• **Place your blocks on a design wall.**
It doesn't have to be anything fancy, but should be a material to which the blocks cling without being pinned. I use a king-size, flat flannel sheet, which I tack to the wall. Other possibilities include cotton batting or a flannel-backed vinyl table cloth. If you don't have a large wall space, you might consider covering foam-core boards with flannel. These rigid flannel surfaces can be propped against a piece of furniture to allow you adequate design space.
• **Try out many different sets.**
Start with a tangent, straight set. Stand back and look at the arrangement. Move the blocks into a tangent, diagonal set. Separate the blocks, as if to insert strips of sashing. For now, the flannel can serve as the sashing and give you an idea of how the quilt will look. Play with each setting possibility. I refer to this process as the "try-outs." It's a design stage during which each setting is "auditioning" for the starring role.
• **Assign adjectives to the layouts while you arrange blocks.**
Using descriptive words like "strong," "feminine," "busy," "soft" or "whimsical" helps me know if I'm on the right track in designing. I even say them out loud so I'll react to them. Avoid value-judgement words like "yucky" or "awesome." They are not helpful in allowing your creativity to flow.
• **Audition fabrics to introduce color.**
Place a fabric you are considering on the wall near the blocks. You may have to pin it because of its bulk. Stand back

and look. Trust your gut instinct. If you don't like it, take it down immediately. If you like it but don't have a sense of "yes," leave it there and try another fabric. I often have up to 10 different fabrics on the wall at one time. If I'm auditioning fabrics for sashing or plain alternating squares, I may end up using lots of different ones. This auditioning process can happen in a few minutes, a few hours, a few days or even over the course of several weeks. Practice patience—you can't rush the creative process. If you're in a hurry, then make quick decisions and don't look back. I learn from every quilt I make. Even design elements I might change the next time are learning experiences.

See the differences for yourself

I enjoy the challenge of doing things differently each time I make a quilt. Even the same setting can look entirely different when the color or scale of the pieces changes.

Compare the photos of "Snow Crystal Express" (page 19) and "Plaid Stars, Rolling Stars" (page 17). I used a 6" finished, triple-lattice sashing with cornerstones in both of them. However, the blocks in "Snow Crystal Express" are set straight while "Plaid Stars, Rolling Stars" has a diagonal set. Also, the triple-lattice sashing in "Snow Crystal Express" has the color values placed in this order: light, dark, light. "Plaid Stars, Rolling Stars" reverses the placement to dark, light, dark. Notice how this simple change makes such a dramatic difference!

"Festival Star" (page 21) also has triple-lattice sashing like that of "Snow Crystal Express"—light, dark, light. However, the varying widths of the strips used in "Festival Star," give it an entirely different feeling. I cut narrow dark strips from many different fabrics, creating a scrappy look and a spacious feel. I also used Four Patch blocks for cornerstones rather than LeMoyne Stars. All three quilts have similar settings, yet each quilt is distinctive and unique.

Some design advice

Think of your quilt as a whole. You want viewers to see the entire quilt first, then experience it one part at a time as they look for interesting things that create a final impression. You want your quilts to have a "long shelf-life." This means that they hold a viewer's attention and there is always something new to discover each time the quilts are seen. Well-designed quilts are those we like to look at over and over again.

Let the quilts in this book inspire you, then challenge yourself to do something different. If you like "Snow Crystal Express" (page 19) because of its red, white and green color recipe as well as its setting, consider making one like it using a different Star block. How would Festival Star blocks look?

Margret Reap asked herself, "How can I use the same framing triangles in a medallion set and make each quilt look different?" Together, we set two different blocks— Star of the Magi and Carpenter's Wheel—in the same setting. Think about color and value as you look at "Star of the Magi Medallion" and "Carpenter's Wheel Medallion" on page 20.

Problem solving

You may find that your blocks are not all the same size. This is a common problem whether you made all of the blocks or had some made by other quiltmakers. Take a close look at "LeMoyne Star and Friends" (page 10). Even though I've been quilting since 1978 and consider myself a very good piecer, the blocks in this sampler quilt varied in their measurements by up to 1/2". You'll be glad to know there are ways to handle this situation.

First, if you cut and piece all the blocks yourself in a relatively short period of time and use the same block pattern, sewing machine and cutting tools, you're more likely to make blocks that are nearly all the same size. Introduce any variable to that equation, and you can anticipate some size discrepancy in the blocks. An easy way to remedy size differences is to frame blocks by sewing fabric strips to each side and then trimming the blocks to the same size. If you want the framing strips to "disappear" visually, use fabric to match the background in the blocks. If you want them to be a visible design element, choose a contrasting fabric or color for emphasis.

I chose contrasting fabric strips for "LeMoyne Star and Friends." You might think that doing so would cause the difference in the widths of the frames to become noticeable. However, there are so many things for viewers to look at in this quilt that the slight difference in the light strips is negligible. In fact, I think the extra sparkle in the quilt gained by adding the light framing strips far outweighs any discrepancy in the frame sizes.

The blocks in the "Northstar" quilt (page 16) came from a Friendship exchange and were different sizes. This time I framed each block in fabric that matched the background. After sewing the strips, I pressed and trimmed the blocks. But take another look. Do you notice anything different about the Northstar blocks in the quilt? The corner accents were not part of the original blocks. After squaring the blocks, I cut the corners and sewed colored triangles to them. The new colors added pizzazz to what might have been an ordinary color recipe. Isn't it nice to know that you can make exciting changes like this even after the blocks are technically finished?

Mastering Y-seaming will move you up the quilters' experience ladder! I hope you pieced lots of small LeMoyne Star blocks for practice and have built a colorful stash of them. By now you've seen how other quilters used the small blocks with larger Star blocks.

Visual stimulation is essential to designing quilts. That's why I've included so many lovely quilt photos for you to enjoy. Designing your own quilts is a liberating feeling and your quilts will "talk" to you if you let them. Just learn to listen. What they say is often heard only in a "gut feeling"—that sense of knowing when something is working or not. Enjoy the setting process and reap the rewards!

- Use A templates for 6" LeMoyne Star blocks and for Star blocks measuring 12".

- Use B templates for 5 1/8" LeMoyne Star blocks and for Star blocks measuring 10 1/4".

- Step-by-step directions and how-to photos for cutting and piecing a LeMoyne Star block begin on page 5.

- General directions and piecing diagrams for all Star blocks begin on page 11.

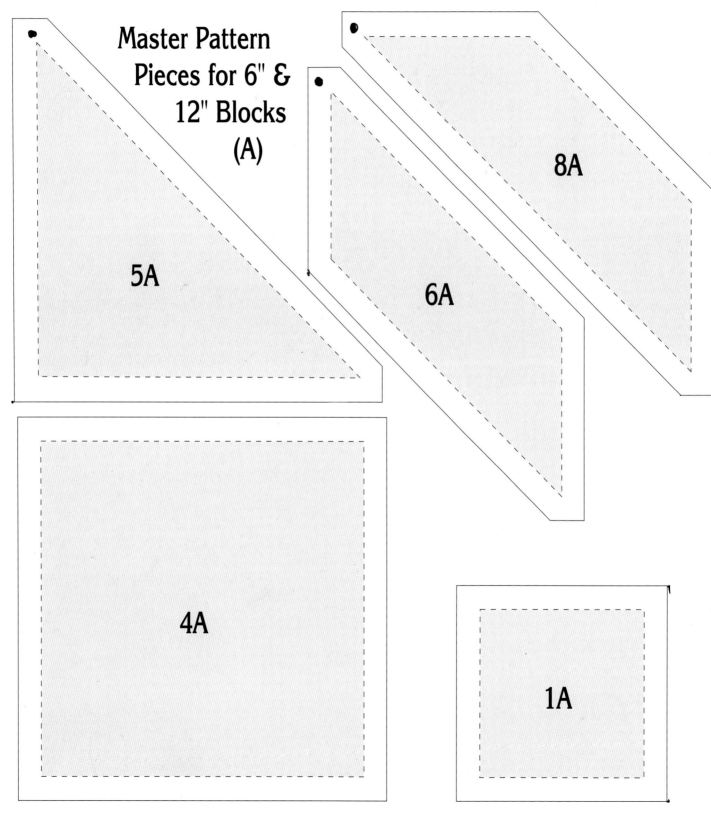

Master Pattern Pieces for 6" & 12" Blocks (A)

5A

8A

6A

4A

1A

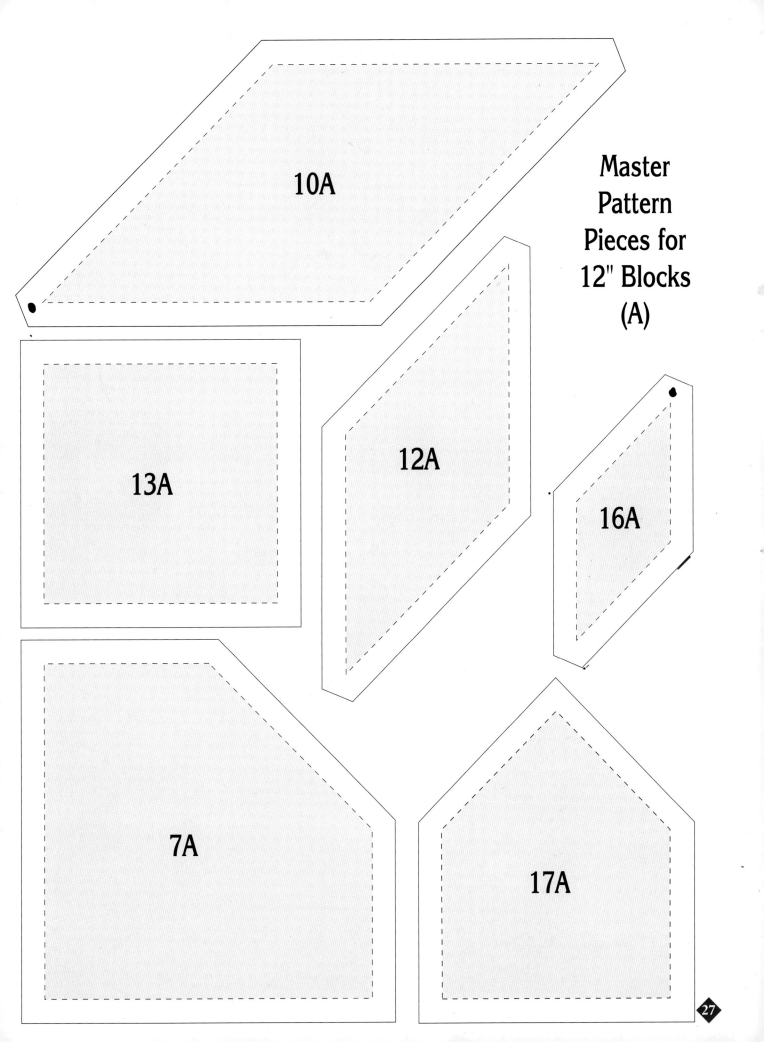

10A

Master
Pattern
Pieces for
12" Blocks
(A)

13A

12A

16A

7A

17A

27

Master Pattern Pieces for 12" Blocks (A)

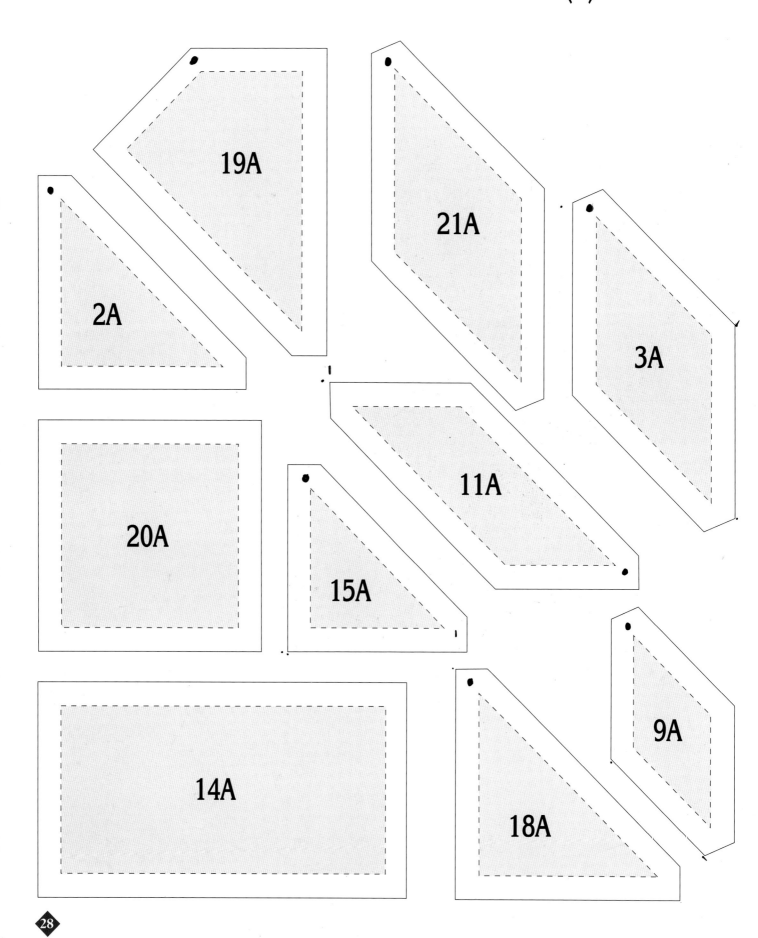

Master Pattern Pieces for 5 1/8" & 10 1/4" Blocks (B)

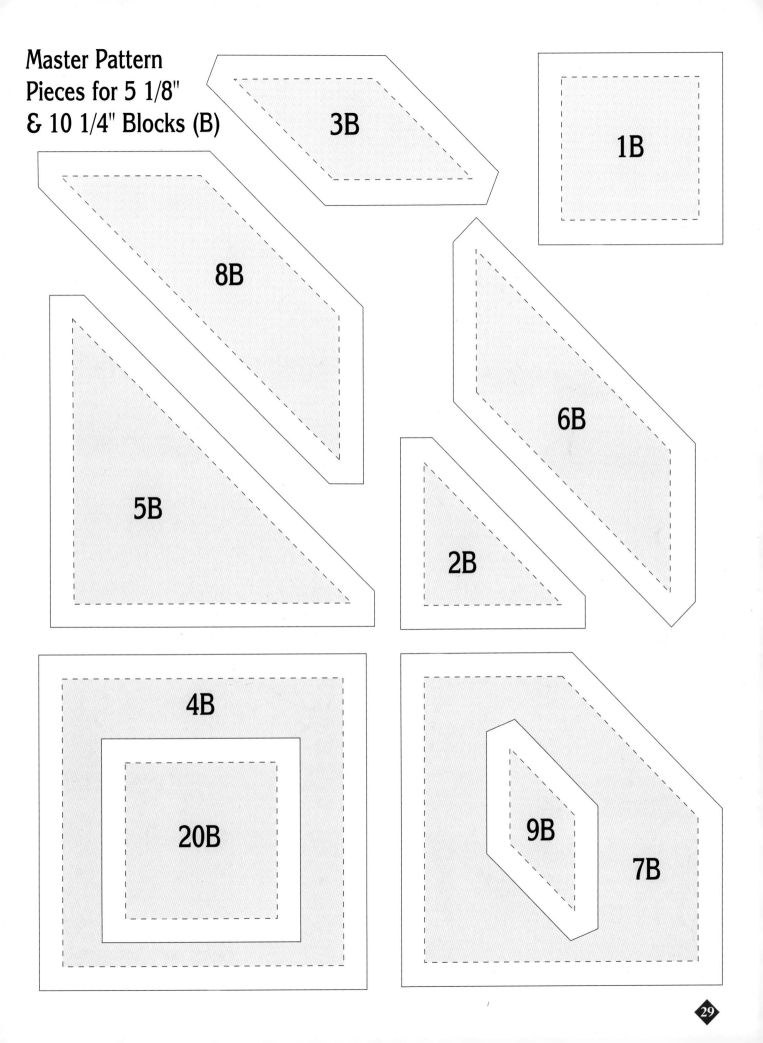

3B

1B

8B

5B

6B

2B

4B

20B

9B

7B

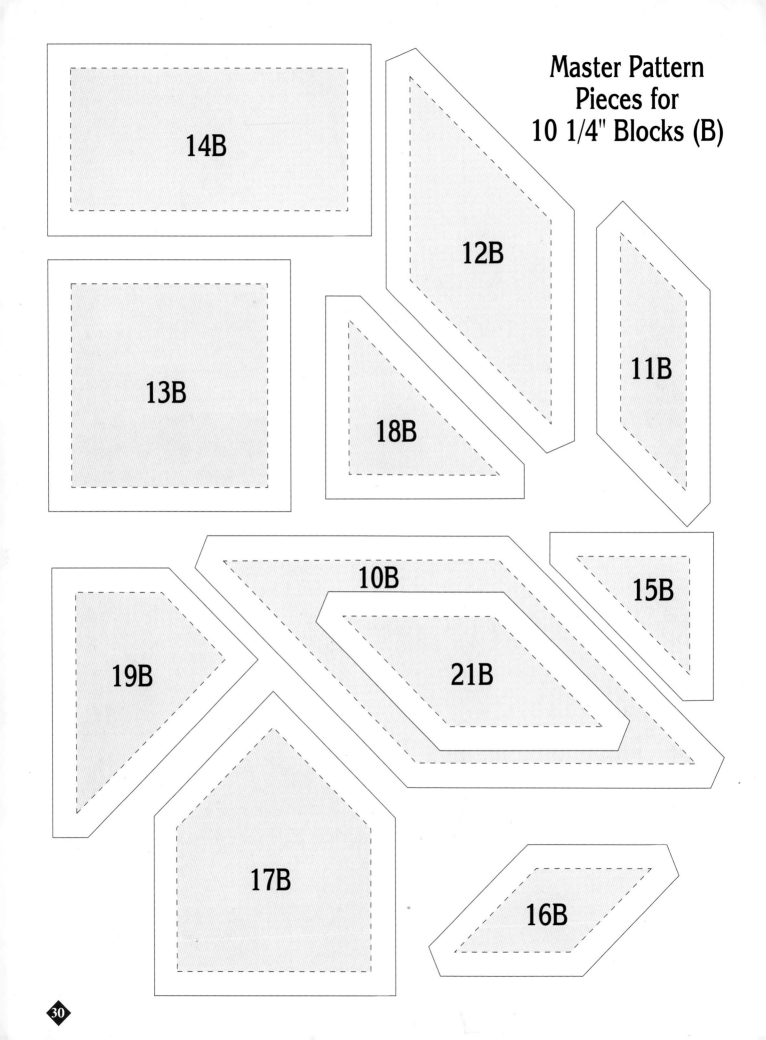

Master Pattern
Pieces for
10 1/4" Blocks (B)

14B

12B

13B

11B

18B

10B

15B

19B

21B

17B

16B

30

CHAPTER 5

Learn to Draft Blocks in Any Size

Do you want to make blocks in other sizes? You'll be glad to know there is a simple way to make blocks in any size you choose. All you need is a calculator, a "magic number" and an easy formula. There are two ways to approach the drafting—Method 1 (choosing a finished block size) and Method 2 (choosing a pattern piece size that's easy to work with). I used Method 1 to make the pattern pieces for the 12" blocks and Method 2 for the 10 1/4" blocks.

UNDERSTANDING "MAGIC NUMBERS"

LeMoyne Stars belong to a category of blocks known as eight-pointed stars. This category of blocks is based on equal division of a circle into eight pie-shaped wedges with 45° angles. One characteristic of blocks in this category is that they are often partially composed of true diamonds. By definition a diamond has four equal sides and two pairs of parallel sides.

When you look at the LeMoyne Star block, notice that the side of a diamond is equal to the side of a square. It is also equal to the side of the triangle. So, if you knew the actual measurement of any one of these three pieces, you would know the sizes of the other two pieces.

According to the Pythagorean Theorem we know that the diagonal of a square equals 1.414 times its side measurement. Therefore, the diagonal of the triangle that you see on the LeMoyne Star is 1.414 times its side measurement because the triangle is one-half of a square. When you total the parts that fit along one side of the block's outer edge, you get 3.414. You can use this "magic number" and a calculator to determine the sizes of the pattern pieces for any size LeMoyne Star block. If you prefer, you can choose the finished size of the pattern pieces and then determine the size of the block.

Method 1
- Choose a finished block size.
- Divide the block size by the "magic number" (3.414) to get the side measurement of the square, diamond and triangle. Round that number up to the nearest 1/8".
- Add 1/4" seam allowances to all sides to determine what size to cut the pieces.

EXAMPLE:

Finished block size	÷ Magic number	=Finished size of pieces
8"	÷ 3.414	=2.343" (2 3/8")

Method 2
- Choose a finished size for the pattern pieces that's easy to cut.
- Multiply that number by the "magic number" (3.414) to determine the finished block size. Round that number up to the nearest 1/8".

EXAMPLE:

Finished size of pieces	x Magic number	=Finished block size
2"	x 3.414	=6.828" (6 7/8")

While the finished block size may seem odd, 2" pattern pieces are an easy size to cut. If your entire quilt is made using the same size blocks, then it makes no difference what size they measure. Knowing the block size will be helpful when cutting setting triangles though, if you use the blocks in a diagonal set.

Using the formula for other blocks
Once you know how to use the "magic number" for LeMoyne Star blocks, you can use the same formula for some of the more complex Star blocks. For example, let's look at the

1+   1.414+   1= 3.414

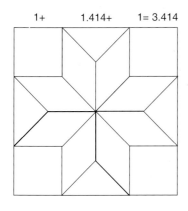

12" Morning Star block. When you divide 12" by 3.414, you'll find that the side measurement of the square and triangle is 3 1/2". However, two small diamonds fit along the side of the square and the triangle, so you need to divide 3 1/2" by 2 to find the size of the small diamonds.

Wheel, you'll need to total the parts which fit along one outside edge of the block to come up with a new magic number. Then use it in the formula as before.

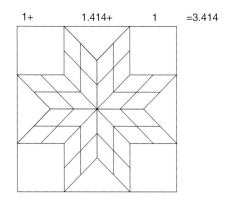

| 1+ | 1.414+ | 1 | =3.414 |

EXAMPLE:			
Finished block size	÷ Magic number	=Square & Triangle	÷ 2=Diamonds
12"	÷ 3.414	=3.5	÷ 2=1.75"

| 1+ | 1+ | 1.414+ | 1.414+ | 1+ | 1 | =6.828 |

EXAMPLE:		
Finished block size	÷ Magic number	=Finished size of pieces
12"	÷ 6.828	=1.75"

Finding a new "magic number"

For complex blocks with more pieces, such as the Carpenter's

That's all there is to using "magic numbers" for drafting the LeMoyne Star block and all its friends!

Other Books by Sharyn Craig

- ◆ Designing New Traditions In Quilts
- ◆ Twist 'n Turn
- ◆ Design Challenge: Pyramids Plus!
- ◆ The Ultimate Half Log Cabin

For ordering information, contact:
Chitra Publications, 2 Public Avenue, Montrose, PA 18801
Website, www.QuiltTownUSA.com;
Phone (800)628-8244 or (570)278-6335; Fax (570)278-2223
or E-mail: chitraws@epix.net